3.93
oop
4|07

Don't Make Me Laugh

**How to feel better about
living with a weak bladder**
written by Nicky Asbury & Helen White

Acknowledgments

Special thanks to Dr Paul Smith, Consultant Clinical Psychologist at Northumbria Health Care NHS Trust for his inspiration, Jen Craig, Kathryn Dickson and Caroline Jobey at North Tyneside Hospital for their administrative support, Heather Welford for her careful editing, Kate Welford for her creative designing, our colleagues at the Northumbria Healthcare NHS Trust, the Continence Foundation, members of *In*contact, and most of all, to all the women who generously shared their experiences and helped us to prepare this guide.

Cartoons by Dennis Parrack

ISBN 0-9541418-0-6

Published by:

Northumbria Healthcare NHS Trust
North Tyneside General Hospital
Rake Lane
North Shields
Tyne & Wear
NE29 8NH

Printed by Statex Colourprint, Newcastle upon Tyne

This Guide has been printed with the support of:

Northumbria Healthcare **NHS**
NHS Trust

sanofi~synthelabo

The
Continence
Foundation

Contents

Foreword

Introduction

1 Can't jump, daren't run

2 Helping your bladder, helping yourself

3 I'm OK as I am

4 Me, Myself and I

5 Go with the flow

6 Here's looking at you

7 Blues and loos

8 Anxiety, panic and worry

9 Love me, love my bladder

Who can help

To boldly go

Further reading

Diaries and Charts

Foreword

Welcome to the weak bladder club . . . you're in good company. Now I'm nearing 40, I can't even go three stops on the motorway after a Diet Coke without pulling over. For me it's my prostate, for you it's your bladder or your pelvic floor. And there's a lot of it about. Leaking a bit when coughing, laughing or exercising is very common (14% of women and 6.6% of men over 30 are or have been incontinent) but it remains a taboo. 75% of sufferers won't discuss it with their partner and 30% won't trouble the GP. According to a recent Gallup poll, that makes us the most embarrassed nation in Europe.

The same survey also found out that for 5% of women, the doctor's embarrassment was a major problem preventing them from seeking medical treatment. Mercifully, all newly qualified doctors and GPs now receive communication skills training and should be able to discuss embarrassing problems without turning bright puce and palming it off on the practice nurse. But if you're still unconvinced, head straight for the nurse. The bottom line is that a lot of help is available if you know where to find it, so don't suffer in silence. This guide is an excellent starting point. Not only does it deal with the specific problems of how your bladder does (or doesn't) work, but it takes a very holistic view. Dealing with the psychological impact of any problem is often the key to success. So help your bladder and help yourself . . .

Phil Hammond

Dr Phil Hammond

Salome's Story

I'm Salome, born in Kenya, brought up on the northwest coast of Scotland and now living in Newcastle with my partner, Edward.

I've had a weak bladder for over 10 years. As a young girl I was fit and healthy, an outdoor sporty person, keen on athletics and mountaineering, art and music. I led an active life.

I was in my early 20's working with young people when I realised I had real difficulties going to the loo. Once in a blue moon I would wet the bed if I was really stressed, such as exam times, but now I was having to pay special attention to my personal hygiene.

I continued to struggle on supporting myself through college. No parents, partner or financial support, I was barely surviving. I finished my degree course and worked part-time, but the money I earned covered my travel and little else, such as the mounting student debts waiting to be repaid.

My incontinence became a real factor in my life, no money, or washing machine, I was hand washing sheets and sleeping on the floor because it took days to get the mattress dry. My bladder was out of control. I had a nervous breakdown. The medication affected my body image; I became fat, couldn't concentrate, or keep myself clean.

Then I met Edward. He never condemned me about my accidents, nor got annoyed when I was rushing to the loo just as we were going out. He made me realise I had a health, not a moral problem! Having been brought up with the old fashioned view that wetting yourself was degrading, being out of control, regressing to childhood, I tended to be harsh with myself - can't even go without damp knickers.

He encouraged me to join the *"Don't make me laugh"* project. The Guide has helped me to survive. I am not looking back, as it gave me the confidence to see my doctor. I left uplifted. My time doing pelvic floor exercises with the physiotherapist has been real therapy, and made me realise I'm not on my own.

I'm not cured, but I'm not looking back. Instead of being afraid, I get a little more upbeat each day. I feel proud of myself and what I have achieved, and one day I'd like to start a family.

So please, don't give up hope. Life needn't be a wet blanket. Don't give up seeking help.

Yours with goodwill

Salome

Salome

Introduction to the guide

Why do we need this Guide? A major reason is that one in three women (and one in ten men) have to deal with continence problems, but fewer than half of them seek help from their GP, nurse or continence advisor. The reasons women give are:

- They have too little time.
- They don't see it as a serious enough problem.
- It's not worth bothering their GP with.
- They don't have enough information about treatment options.
- They don't feel treatment will work.
- They manage well themselves.

However, as well as practical explanations, there are emotional reasons:

- Women find it embarrassing and shameful.
- They fear they won't be taken seriously.
- They fear surgery is the only option.

Anxiety, worry, low mood and low self-esteem are the most common emotions women say their weak bladder causes.

The Guide is aimed at:

- Women who are distressed and haven't yet sought help
- Women who are living with long-term bladder problems
- Women who want to try some new ways to manage their emotional reactions
- Women who feel they can manage their physical symptoms but want to promote their well-being.

The Guide contains information about the physical aspects of a weak bladder, but its main sections are aimed at helping you develop new ways of dealing with the most common emotional problems.

Accessing health professionals is included in 'Who Can help' on page 63. If you prefer to discuss your problems with others you may find a consumer group is helpful. Again details are in this section.

Nicky Asbury & Helen White
Northumbria Healthcare NHS Trust

Can't jump, daren't run

How your bladder works

When the bladder is beginning to feel full (with about 1/2 a pint of fluid), signals are sent to the brain. The brain responds and the bladder muscles contract, squeezing out the urine. At the same time the muscles at the bladder outlet (the urethra) relax, allowing the urine to pass from the body.

There are three common conditions known as a 'weak bladder':

Genuine stress incontinence

Urge incontinence

Mixed incontinence.

Genuine stress incontinence

Genuine stress incontinence is often known simply as stress incontinence, and it's not to be confused with emotional stress.

The bladder, uterus (womb) and bowel are supported by a sling of muscles called the pelvic floor muscles. These muscles may begin to sag during pregnancy, following an operation, or after the menopause due to hormonal changes. When we laugh, run, sneeze or do any physical movement, we put extra pressure on these muscles. This causes urine to leak out, because the muscles aren't able to keep supporting the bladder outlet correctly.

Women only have one urethral sphincter (men have two, an internal and an external

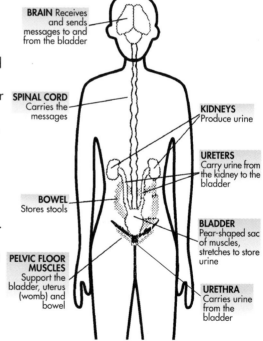

BRAIN Receives and sends messages to and from the bladder

SPINAL CORD Carries the messages

KIDNEYS Produce urine

URETERS Carry urine from the kidney to the bladder

BOWEL Stores stools

BLADDER Pear-shaped sac of muscles, stretches to store urine

PELVIC FLOOR MUSCLES Support the bladder, uterus (womb) and bowel

URETHRA Carries urine from the bladder

sphincter). This is a ring of muscles surrounding the urethra and it helps to hold in and release urine from the bladder. If the sphincter is damaged during childbirth, it's not able to squeeze as tightly to hold in the urine, and leaks may result.

The most popular and effective treatment for stress incontinence is to strengthen the pelvic floor muscles by pelvic floor exercises. These are usually taught by a specially trained physiotherapist or nurse. They can be done while standing waiting for a bus, sitting watching TV, relaxing in the bath or cleaning your teeth. You don't have to lie on the floor.

How to do pelvic floor exercises

Firstly, identify the correct muscles. Imagine you're trying to stop yourself passing wind by squeezing the muscles around your back passage. Can you feel these move? This is the back part of your pelvic floor. Now imagine you're about to pass urine and squeeze up these muscles to stop the flow. Can you feel these move? This is the front part of your pelvic floor.

Judy stopped going to aerobics when she found she wet herself doing star jumps. One night she confided to her husband what had happened and she was worried in case she would leak during their love-making. He was very sympathetic and persuaded her to ring the Continence Foundation Helpline number they had seen in a magazine article. The Helpline nurse was reassuring and encouraged Judy to get help from her practice nurse.

The muscles in your thighs and tummy should remain relaxed as you tighten and relax the pelvic floor muscles.

Slow pull-ups: slowly tighten and pull up these muscles as hard as you can for as long as you can - count how many seconds you can hold on for - now relax.
Fast pull-ups: pull up the muscles quickly and tightly and then relax immediately. Repeat five fast and five slow pull-ups as often as you can - at least 10 times a day.

It may take some weeks before you begin to feel the benefits. As your muscles become stronger, they squeeze tighter.

Keep exercising several times each day, forever.

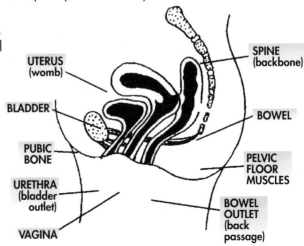

Some women find using a vaginal cone helps. The cones are made of plastic or metal, in a range of weights; one is placed in the vagina for about fifteen minutes twice a day. You have to try to hold it in during that time. Start with the lightest weight, gradually building up to a heavier weight.

You may be advised to have a few sessions of electro-stimulation. A small probe is inserted into your vagina and a low-grade electrical current is passed through the muscles. This helps you to become aware of the correct muscles and to start the strengthening process. It's not a painful treatment.

Other treatment options
An operation to repair the weakened muscles might be advised if other treatments aren't appropriate or haven't been successful. The Continence Foundation Helpline can send you a fact sheet, 'Surgery for Stress Incontinence in Women' (see page 65). Your doctor may refer you to a urogynaecologist, a specialist surgeon.

Urge incontinence (overactive bladder)

This means the bladder needs to be emptied frequently - more often than every two hours and twice or more at night, often as the result of a sudden urge, and with only small amounts of urine. You may find you're wet before you've reached the loo.

Bladder exercises (bladder retraining)
These train the bladder to 'hang on'. Before beginning them, keep a diary to record each time you pass urine and wet yourself, plus the type and amount of fluid you drink (see pages 71 and 72).

Next, when you have the urge to go, sit down (not only on the toilet at this stage!) and hold on till the urge has passed. Distract yourself by counting up to ten, singing a song or reciting a poem. Then go to the lavatory. You may find as you get nearer to the loo you need to pass water urgently. Sit down and hold on till the urge has passed and then continue to the lavatory.

You'll find you're able to hold on till the time is more convenient. Set yourself realistic goals. If you're dashing to the loo every hour, aim to increase this to an hour and ten minutes, then 15 minutes and so on until you can hold on for a couple of hours or more.

Continue to keep a record, and compare it with your first diary. It may take several weeks to show you've become boss of your bladder.

Biofeedback may be suggested. This is a training programme individually designed for you. Usually combined with pelvic floor exercises.

Medication
Medicines may reduce the urge to pass urine, and can aid your bladder training.

Ditropan XL (Oxybutynin) is the most popular. If you're having side effects, such as a dry mouth, blurred vision or constipation, tell your doctor. (S)he may change your prescription to Detrusitol or Detrunorm, which have a similar action.

Sleeping pills, antidepressants, and blood pressure tablets can affect bladder function. Pain killers containing codeine cause constipation, and this can affect the bladder.

Bladder distension
This means an operation to stretch the bladder. If you have it done, it's important to keep up the bladder exercises afterwards.

Mixed incontinence

Both stress and urge symptoms are known as mixed incontinence. A bladder scan establishes whether you're emptying your bladder completely, and uro-dynamic investigations show how your bladder is filling, and how much it can hold.

Urodynamic tests are normally carried out in the hospital urodynamics department. They aren't painful. You'll be asked to remove your clothes and wear a gown. The whole procedure takes about an hour. For more information, The Continence Foundation factsheet no. 13, 'What is Urodynamics?' is available free from the Continence Foundation (see page 65).

Other common problems

Bladder infections
Infections cause urgency, frequency and pain when passing urine. See your doctor for the appropriate course of antibiotics. Keep drinking plenty of water and take extra care with your personal hygiene.

Cystitis
Cystitis means the bladder is inflamed and causes pain when you pass water. If you have an infection this needs to be treated. You'll be encouraged to drink plenty. Many women find barley water helpful.

Interstitial Cystitis
Although this is less common than cystitis, it presents with some similar symptoms, such as long-term frequency and urgency with pain, temporarily relieved by emptying the bladder. The urine is not infected. At present there's no cure or specific treatment. Some women find changing their diet, and taking medicines such as anti-inflammatory, antihistamine, antispasmodic and muscular relaxants helpful. There is an interstitial cystitis support group (see page 65).

Premenstrual changes
Many women complain their problems increase before a period. Changing hormone patterns can cause a build-up of fluid. This passes once the period starts.

Menopause
Changing hormone levels can cause lax muscles; the vagina may become dry and the urethra may narrow, making it difficult to empty your bladder completely. Hormone tablets or cream can be prescribed.

An obstruction
Constipation or a prolapse at the bladder neck can cause the bladder not to empty completely. This is called overflow and can leave you with the sensation you need to go even after emptying your bladder. You may experience a delay before you can pass urine, or dribbling of urine after you've been. Take time to pass urine and after you've finished, wait a few seconds and then try to pass more. Constipation or straining can cause extra pressure on the bladder or bladder outlet, restricting the flow of urine.

A help-yourself guide to a healthy bladder

Drink plenty - at least 6 mugs or 10 cups of fluid in 24 hours. Water is good and a daily glass of cranberry juice benefits some women. Drink less tea, coffee, cola or alcohol. Drinking with a meal may help, especially in cold weather. Cutting down on drinks can make your urine more concentrated, irritate your bladder, and reduce the amount your bladder can hold.

Eat a balanced diet - more fruit, vegetables and wholemeal bread and fewer cakes and biscuits. This lessens extra strain on your pelvic muscles.

Aim to go to the lavatory regularly four to eight times in 24 hours (every three to four hours). 'Putting off' is as bad as going 'just-in-case'. Going 'just-in-case' leads to frequency and a small bladder capacity.

Take time to empty your bladder completely.

Move your bowels regularly - not necessarily each day. It's the consistency - soft and easy to pass - and not the frequency of the stool that matters.

After a bowel movement wipe your bottom from front to back.

Getting to the lavatory in time

Wear easy-to-manage clothing.

You may find a hand-held urinal specially designed for women a useful solution to difficulties in getting out of bed in time. Your local occupational therapy department or district nurse can advise you.

Try a potty or a commode.

Seeking help

'Information builds up your confidence and makes it easier to seek help' said Jackie, 'I never told anybody.' After years of putting up with being wet, she set about getting help by finding the name of the doctor in her practice who was interested in bladder problems and female. Jackie felt more comfortable talking to a woman.

Increase your confidence by re-reading the beginning of this section; contact a support group, or speak with the Continence Foundation Helpline nurse. If you still find your problems too difficult to talk about, write a note and hand it to your doctor with a list of your symptoms and a copy of your bladder and fluid chart.

What about continence products?
Treatments take time; pads may help you manage your daily life. The type to suit you depends on:

The amount you leak

Your lifestyle

You may decide to pick and mix washable and disposable styles for different occasions - the choice is yours.

The designer-wear range of machine-washable lacy pants with an absorbent pad built into the gusset are becoming as popular as disposable pads for women who leak. Always wash new pants before wearing for the first time. The absorbency improves after the first few washes. Fabric softeners reduce absorbency.

Generally speaking, disposable pads absorb larger quantities and are cheaper than washable pads. However they are bulky to store, and expensive if you're going to need them for a long period.

Both types of pads are available in a variety of shapes, sizes and absorbencies. The appearance and the price of a product don't reflect the quality.

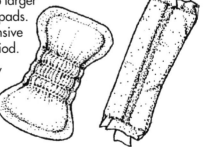

The slimmer disposable pads usually contain a 'gel' for greater absorbency. Start with the smallest pad. If it's not sufficient, try the next size. No pad can be guaranteed leak-free.

Sanitary pads aren't designed to absorb urine, and can cause vaginal dryness. They can also irritate the skin and become smelly. They can be expensive to use long term, as they need changing more frequently.

Washing between your legs, or wiping the area with an alcohol-free moist wipe before replacing a clean pad reduces the risk of stale smells and helps to prevent skin soreness. Seal wet pads in a plastic bag, or in an airtight receptacle and dispose with the normal household waste. Not all pads can be burnt. Store washable pads in a sealed container or soak in a lidded bucket until washed.

New Product News

The PromoCon Helpline can give you the details of the latest products and there's a free guide, 'Choosing products for bladder and bowel control.'

All these products can be bought in major chemists and through mail order. Some Health Trusts supply selected products through their continence service. Your nurse, doctor or continence advisor can advise you. There are specially designed devices (like a tampon) which are placed in the vagina, and which give added support to the neck of your bladder. They can be useful for physical exercise such as aerobics. Discuss with your professional helper.

Protecting the bed

Mattress, pillow case and duvet covers are available in a range of sizes in lightweight, non-rustle water-repellent fabrics.

Out and about with confidence

You'll feel more confident if you plan ahead, and take a few items in a small toilet bag.

- Flushable tissues to fit the toilet seat
- Alcohol-free wipes
- Neat female urinal with drainage bag for the urine
- Spare pants and pads
- Scented bag for soiled pants or pads
- Odour neutraliser
- 'Urgent' card (see next page)
- Bottled water if you're travelling in a hot climate
- RADAR key - The National Key Scheme (NKS) (see next page)

The 'URGENT' card is plastic card which explains you have a medical condition and you need to use the lavatory quickly. It includes the Continence Foundation Helpline number and is available **free** from the Continence Foundation.

The National Key Scheme (NKS) provides you with a key to lavatories which display the RADAR sign, and a NKS Guide gives details of the locations of these lavatories in the UK. You can obtain a key and a copy of the NKS Guide by writing to RADAR and enclosing £3.50 for the key and £5.00 for the Guide. Your cheque or postal order should be made payable to RADAR.

Complementary treatments

If you choose these, seek advice from a professionally qualified therapist. Some therapies women have found useful include aromatherapy, homeopathy, reflexology.

Myths and folklore

In the Middle Ages animal remedies such as a frog tied round the waist were advised for a weak bladder. In the 19th century you had to avoid salt, sharp and sour foods and malt liquor. In the 21st century we continue with our own myths and folklore:

'It's your age . . .' the fact is more women between 25 and 45 years than over 65 have bladder problems

'It's just an inevitable part of being a woman . . .' with the correct treatment, most women can be completely cured, and don't have to accept it as a 'woman's lot'.

'I feel so childlike . . .' incontinence is a recognised medical condition. It can happen to men and women at any age.

'You shouldn't drink after 6pm . . .' there's no scientific evidence to prove restricting drinks prevents you getting up at night.

'An operation will ruin my sex life . . .' you may have to stop having sex for a few weeks after an operation and change your usual love-making positions. Long-term effects aren't inevitable.

'The medicines/treatments didn't work . . .' medicines and treatments are constantly changing. It's always worth asking your doctor 'what's new?'

'My problems started after my hysterectomy . . .' a hysterectomy is performed for a variety of reasons but need not result in bladder problems.

'My weak bladder isn't important enough to bother the doctor . . .' a weak bladder is a genuine medical condition. With the correct treatment most women can be cured or greatly improved.

Good luck!

Helping your bladder, helping yourself

The next sections in the Guide focus on common emotional problems associated with a weak bladder. These are:

- Self-consciousness and social anxiety
- Low self esteem
- Stress
- Negative body image
- Low mood/depression
- Anxiety, panic and worry
- Relationships with other people

Each section includes:

- How the problem can start
- What women say and their experiences
- An action plan with advice

The action plans outlined here are based on the tried and tested methods of cognitive therapy. 'Cognitive' means thought processes and it can refer to a thought, image, memory, belief perception, idea or interpretation. It refers to any of the processes we go through which use our minds, because how we think about a problem often influences what we do about it.

Imagine yourself queuing for the toilet in a shop. If you're able to think 'I'm not in a hurry, I can hold on and the queue's moving quickly' you would probably feel calm and relaxed. You may begin to plan which shop you were going to next or pass the time of day with the person next to you. If, on the other hand your thoughts were 'I'm desperate, I'll have an accident if I don't get there now!' you might feel panicky, annoyed and upset. You might begin to shuffle about and complain people are dawdling and the shop should have better facilities.

What is important here is that the situation is the same. What is different is:

  The perception of the situation

  The meaning or interpretation of the situation

  The effects your thoughts have on your feelings, your body's physical reactions and what you do.

The Distressing Thoughts Action Plan
If we can manage thoughts that are unhelpful it can help us to cope more effectively. Although this won't stop your bladder problems, it can stop your bladder getting you down.

1. How to identify mood changes
Our moods and feelings change constantly as a reaction to what is happening around us. Naming the mood or emotion can be useful because it tunes us into our thoughts and from there we can work out what to do next.

2. How to identify thoughts linked to moods
'Thinking about our thinking' is a skill we can learn with practice. Thoughts enter our minds quickly, automatically and often seem not to be connected to each other. This means we can exclude or filter out thoughts or ideas, which are new or unusual. So if we are low or anxious we pay more attention to sad and worrying thoughts and rule out thoughts that could make us feel better.

TRY THIS! Catching thoughts

If you find it difficult to catch hold of your thoughts, try to answer the questions in the summary box below.

QUESTIONS TO ASK

What was going through my mind immediately before I felt like this?

What was I doing?

What were other people around me saying or doing?

If you find it hard to catch your thoughts when you're low or anxious:

- Begin just by thinking about your thinking when you're doing your normal daily activities.
- Try to catch positive changes in your mood and the thoughts that go with them.
- Write them down.

It can be difficult seeing your most fearful or embarrassing thoughts in black and white, but the goal of writing thoughts down is to help you see them as they really are: thoughts, not facts. You wouldn't expect yourself to remember a full week's shopping list, so why try it with other important thoughts?

TRY THIS! Keeping a diary of events, moods and thoughts

Notice the next time you feel your mood has changed. Describe in as much detail as you can the event or situation you were involved in.

- Give the mood a name.
- Write down all the thoughts that come into your mind - everything, whether it seems important or not.

A blank chart is provided in the Charts section on page 69 of the guide (distressing thoughts diary) You can write down any other details you think are important too. Once you've identified the thoughts, check out whether the thinking style is unhelpful.

3. Ten Types of Unhelpful Thinking Styles

TRY THIS! Recognising unhelpful thinking styles

We've never met anyone, including ourselves, who hasn't at some point said, 'Ah! I do that!'

1. All or nothing thinking Seeing the world in black and white. People are all good or all bad, nothing will ever be the same again, or things will never change.

Elizabeth stopped going to her aerobics class when her weak bladder got more severe. She thought 'my bladder stops me doing everything I enjoy! I can't do anything anymore.' It may be true that some activities feel restricted but this thought stopped Elizabeth looking for a solution to the problem or an alternative activity she could do.

2. Over-generalization This involves believing that because an event has happened it will happen again and again.

Jennifer was unable to get to the toilet in time because of a queue and said to herself 'I'm not going to that shop again, there's always a queue.' Consequently she never checked whether this was the busiest toilet in town or whether she just hit it at lunchtime on a Saturday when it is always busy.

3. *Mental filter* Picking out the negative detail and dwelling on it. By excluding other information we then think the whole situation is negative.

Julie's friend told her she liked her new perfume. Julie told herself 'I bet she's noticed I smell of urine and is relieved the perfume hides it.' In fact the friend just liked the new perfume and wanted to but some for herself.

4. *Disqualifying the positive* Putting down achievements, accomplishments and successes to luck, chance or someone else and rejecting compliments or pats on the back.

Marion's ex-husband had been cruel and insensitive about her weak bladder, refusing to cuddle her after sex if she had leaked, and insisting that she changed the sheets. She told herself 'I'll never be able to have another relationship again. Men are all the same.' She was filtering out the fact she knew other friends whose husbands were supportive with their weak bladders, and her ex-husband was mean to all women he knew.

5. *Jumping to conclusions* This is a case of 2 + 2 = 5, jumping to an explanation when the facts don't add up. There are two types:

Ann thought her friend Moira was tired of her constant requests to go to the toilet and began to see herself as a nuisance. She decided not to go on the shopping trip they had planned to avoid irritating Moira. The reality was Moira was very disappointed as she was looking forward to the day out, and didn't find Ann a nuisance at all.

Mind reading - we guess or assume what other people are thinking and treat it as a fact.

Fortune telling - we predict things will go wrong when they haven't even happened yet. This can stop us preparing ways to cope, if the situation does happen. It also puts us off getting into the situation. The eventual result can be avoidance and isolation.

Pat told herself she would not be able to ask for toilet stops on her Women's Institute trip and therefore cancelled her place.

6. Magnifying (catastrophising) and minimising When we think about the future we predict a disaster. When we manage something, we minimise it so much we'd need a microscope to see it, and assume others won't have noticed it.

When Kate got home from work she realised her pad had leaked on her skirt. She felt embarrassed and assumed everyone at work and on the bus had noticed. She did not take into account she was examining the skirt under bright lights at home, had been wearing her coat on the bus, or people at work had been too busy doing their own tasks to notice the small patch.

7. Emotional reasoning Assuming that because we feel a certain way it must mean we are a certain way.

Karen reasoned, 'I feel unattractive and therefore I must be unattractive.' Relying on thoughts as facts stops us looking at the whole picture.

8. Shoulds, oughts and musts Sometimes 'shoulds', 'oughts' and 'musts' act as impossible standards for us to reach. This can lead us to feeling guilty, frustrated and angry.

Sue felt upset when she told herself 'I shouldn't go to the toilet so often. I must wait or I'll never get my work finished.' By trying to stick to her self-set rules she was putting herself under unnecessary pressure.

9. Labelling and mislabelling Labelling yourself a 'failure' because of something that goes wrong has a much more distressing effect than saying to yourself 'I made a mistake'.

Eileen ordered the wrong pads. She told herself 'I'm pathetic and useless.' In fact she could have told herself the form was complicated and it was the first time she'd completed it. There was no problem sending them back anyway.

10. Personalization Taking on board all responsibility for something happening when it isn't under your control.

Teresa stopped going to her physio because she felt her pelvic floor exercises weren't working. She personalised the problem and said to herself: 'I'm not doing them properly. It's my own fault I leak, the physio's done everything she can!'

Another natural break!

If you find an unhelpful thinking style, add it to the diary and go on to the next stage.

4. Challenging unhelpful thoughts

Viewing the situation in a new way takes a lot of effort. If you find it hard to begin with, ask a partner or friend to help.

TRY THIS! Challenging thoughts

First of all, pick out one thought.
Imagine putting this thought 'on trial', in the witness box. Will it stand up to being questioned?

You can use the questions below to help:

QUESTIONS TO ASK

- Is my thought 100% accurate? What does the thinking style I've identified tell me?
- If this thought were true, what would that mean to me? Is it as important as I am treating it? How will I feel about it next week? What would a partner or friend say about this?
- What would a friend or relative think if this were happening to them?
- If they were thinking like I am now what would I say to them to help them feel better?
- Are there factors in the situation that I'm overlooking or discounting?
- When situations have happened like this before, what have I done to help me? What did I do to cope then? What can I use from that experience to help me cope now?
- Am I jumping to conclusions or mind reading?
- Am I overlooking strengths I have that can help me solve the problem?

5. Finding a balanced view

Finding a balanced view doesn't involve replacing a negative thought with a positive one. Instead, it gives you a fuller picture and explanation of why the situation is that way.

Putting it all together - Molly's Story

> **Molly is 52, and had experienced the symptoms of stress incontinence since her mid 30s. Since the menopause she had developed some new symptoms of urgency, and was finding these more troublesome. One afternoon her daughter found Molly tearful and describing herself as 'fed up'.**

1. Identifying mood changes

When Molly considered it further she recognised she felt anxious, puzzled, angry and down. She felt puzzled because she didn't know why she felt anxious. She was angry with herself for feeling this way.

2. Identifying thoughts linked to moods

Molly checked out the summary box questions and wrote the following on a diary.

EVENT/SITUATION	FEELINGS	THOUGHTS
About 2pm got a call from friend Susan who let me know she'd got tickets for us to go to the theatre.	Anxious	I'll never last the length of that play without the loo. She never said where the tickets were for. I bet it's the middle of a row. That will be impossible for me.
	Puzzled	Why do I feel so anxious?
	Angry	My bladder rules my life. It's not fair!
	Down	I've wanted to see this play for ages, but I won't be able to manage and enjoy it. I'll have to tell her I can't go.

When Molly wrote down the thoughts it became apparent why she felt the way she did.

3. Finding the unhelpful thinking styles

Molly then checked out whether there were any unhelpful thinking styles which were making her feel worse.

EVENT/SITUATION	FEELINGS	THOUGHTS	UNHELPFUL THINKING STYLE
About 2pm got a phone call from friend Susan who said she'd got tickets for the theatre.	Anxious	I'll never last the length of that play without the loo.	**All or nothing thinking**
		She never said where the tickets were.	**Mind reading**
		I bet it's in the middle of a row. That will be impossible for me!	**Catastrophizing**
	Puzzled	Why do I feel so anxious?	
	Angry	My bladder rules my life. It's not fair!	
	Down	I've wanted to see this play for ages, but I won't be able to manage and enjoy it. I'll have to tell her I can't go.	**Fortune telling**

Molly began to see how her initial reaction was catastrophic. She answered the question of why she felt anxious, 'because I'm thinking everything will go wrong' and this reduced her puzzled feelings and her anxiety. Her angry feelings did not have an unhelpful thinking style she could identify. In fact she was letting her bladder rule her and having the problem did not seem fair. She went on to challenge her thoughts by answering the questions in the summary box.

Molly realised the thoughts were based on her anxieties about having to push past people in the row at the theatre and there were some solutions to the problem. Molly realised she hadn't even checked where the seats were, and she could change them if necessary. Her daughter also pointed out the last time Molly had been to the theatre she had only got up once more than Susan! Molly completed the final column and then rang Susan back to work out a solution.

EVENT/SITUATION	FEELINGS	THOUGHTS	UNHELPFUL THINKING STYLE	ALTERNATIVE THOUGHTS
About 2pm got a phone call from friend Susan who let me know she'd got tickets for us to go to the theatre.	Anxious	I'll never last the length of that play without the loo. She never said where the tickets were for. I bet it's the middle of a row. That will be impossible for me!	**All or nothing thinking** **Mind reading** **Catastrophiazing**	I may need the loo but I can go prepared. I can check where the tickets are for. If it is the middle we we could try to change them for the side. It may be difficult but it's not impossible, I can find a way around it.
	Puzzled	Why do I feel so anxious?		
	Angry	My bladder rules my life. It's not fair.		I am letting my bladder rule my life. I need to find some new ways of looking at this.
	Down	I've been wanting to see this play for ages, but I won't be able to manage and enjoy it. I'll have to tell her I can't go.	**Fortune telling**	I can manage. I will find a way. I will tell Susan my worries, she'll understand.

Molly didn't solve the problem of needing the toilet during the play but by viewing the situation differently, she opened up the options. Her distressing feelings reduced and she gained confidence by tackling the problem. Checking out situations gives us options and then our usual coping methods get a chance to come to the fore.

How self-consciousness starts

Self-consciousness starts if we think we're different, unacceptable, or unusual. We think the differences mean other people will judge us badly. Human beings like to belong, and we do this by being similar. Feeling we're different makes us uncomfortable. Because no one talks about bladders (or bowels) it means we never know we share the problem with millions of other women. Knowing you aren't alone can be comforting and reassuring.

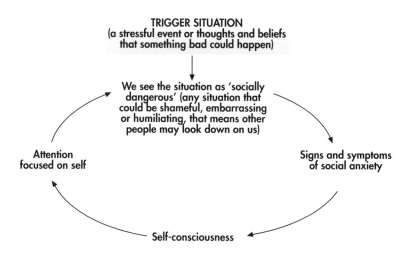

TRIGGER SITUATION
(a stressful event or thoughts and beliefs that something bad could happen)

We see the situation as 'socially dangerous' (any situation that could be shameful, embarrassing or humiliating, that means other people may look down on us)

Attention focused on self

Signs and symptoms of social anxiety

Self-consciousness

What is self-consciousness?

When we become self-conscious we focus our attention on ourselves rather than on anything else. This can be on physical discomfort such as racing heart if we are anxious, or blushing if we are embarrassed. The more our attention focuses on ourselves the more we think our inadequacies are on view to the world, and this makes us think others are even more likely to look down on us.

Often, for women with a weak bladder it's not an actual event (such as wetting themselves or a leak) that causes the self-consciousness but fear of this happening. The thought itself is a trigger for self-consciousness.

Typical trigger situations for women with a weak bladder are:

Fear of accidents and leaking

Fear of smelling or staining

Fear of other people finding out.

Often the worst predictions don't happen because we go to great lengths to perform 'safety behaviours' - so-called because they're designed to help us feel safe and in control.

Sadly, one of the ways we prevent self-consciousness is by withdrawing from other people. Although this reduces feelings of worry, it can make us feel isolated, and even more concerned about other people's view of us.

The first stage in managing self-consciousness is to work out if there's any 'real danger' in a situation. Next we have to check out what triggered the self-consciousness.

Following the distressing thoughts action plan is the first stage. (see page 10)

1. Identify the mood change. As well as 'self-conscious', are you experiencing other feelings?

2. Identify the thoughts linked to moods. What were you doing before you became self-conscious?

This could help you to identify a trigger for your change in mood and shift in focus from outside yourself to onto yourself.

3. Check out unhelpful thinking styles (on page 15)
Michelle was chatting in the pub when a friend commented she was the only one wearing a skirt.

Michelle's diary is outlined below:

EVENT/SITUATION	EMOTION	THOUGHTS	BEHAVIOUR
In the pub on a Friday night a friend commented I was the only one wearing a skirt.	*Self-conscious. Embarrassed. Upset.*	*They know it's because I've got a pad on. Everyone is staring at me and thinking I'm stupid. I'm not like the others, I don't fit in.*	*Became tearful Made an excuse and left early.*

Michelle's immediate thoughts were very distressing but she went on to find alternative explanations:

THOUGHTS	UNHELPFUL THINKING STYLES	ALTERNATIVE BALANCED THOUGHTS
They know it's because I've got a pad on.	*Mind reading.*	*How can they know that! They can't see and I've not told them.*
Everyone's staring at me. They think I'm stupid.	*All or nothing.* *Mind reading.*	*No they aren't. Sandra's just gone to the loo, Louise is looking at that bloke at the bar and Wendy's just been searching her handbag for lipstick! Someone commenting I'm wearing a skirt does not mean they think I'm stupid.*
I'm not like the others. I don't fit in.	*Over generalising.*	*Maybe I'm not like the others tonight because I am the only one in a skirt, but I'm like the others in lots of other ways.*

This helped by distracting her from her embarrassment, blushing and tears. These sensations had become a source of self-consciousness themselves. Although Michelle was still focusing on her thoughts she was actively looking for ways to feel better. She felt calmer and got back into the conversation. This helped reduce her sense of being different.

One of the main things we know about self-consciousness and social anxiety is that although a woman may see herself as different to others, other women don't share the view. Taking an alternative look at ourselves can help here. Think about ways in which you are similar to others, and make a list.

Immediate coping strategies

1. Stop Excessive Checking
Although checking works in the short term, it means we are focusing more attention on ourselves and keeps self-consciousness going.

TRY THIS! *A quick check*
Allow yourself one quick body check. Start at the top of your head and gradually move down your body to your feet. Tell yourself you are okay then focus on what's happening around you, or someone you're with.

2. Calm physical symptoms
Being self-conscious is usually accompanied by the symptoms of anxiety, such as trembling, shaking and blushing. Use the quick calming techniques outlined on page 35. Practise this even when you aren't self-conscious, to become more confident about it.

3. Take the heat off yourself
Shift your attention away from yourself and back onto what's happening around you. Find an object in the middle distance and notice every detail about it. If your attention slips back onto yourself, find something else to dwell on.

4. Shift your focus
For example, if you're suddenly aware of your pad/dampness concentrate on the warmth of your right hand or your foot in your shoe. If you notice the symptoms of embarrassment, remind yourself it will soon pass and focus on using the calming techniques on page 34 - 35.

5. Shift your attention from yourself to someone else.
If you're self-conscious when someone pays you attention, and looking them in the eye is difficult, look at their ears or forehead. Use this time to calm yourself before responding.

Two women's stories

Rachel

Rachel, now aged 42, had grown up the youngest and much-wanted girl in a family of five boys. She had always felt her parents and brothers wanted her to be pretty, feminine and attractive and was praised and valued in the family for how she looked and her appearance. She was expected to be quiet and polite in contrast to her noisy, boisterous brothers. She began to live by the rule 'unless I am attractive other people won't like me'. She wasn't directly aware that this was a belief she had, but she found herself feeling down or worried if she ever acted or thought in a way that seemed to go against this. She remembered her parents' resistance to her wishes to having her hair cut short and their dismay and disapproval when she did.

Over the previous two years Rachel realised she was constantly dashing to the loo and getting up three or four times a night. Her pants were frequently damp and she worried she smelled. She told herself: 'I'm old and ugly. No-one will want me'. As far as she was concerned she couldn't be attractive with a condition she felt was disgusting. She assumed that other people would find her disgusting and dislike her. She gradually withdrew from friendships and activities she had enjoyed and became low in mood as a result of seeing herself so negatively.

Anne

Anne is married, aged 64, and had a part time job in a local school as well as looking after her two young granddaughters. She had always prided herself on her ability to take problems in her stride and cope with life's challenges. She was always on the go and had a good relationship and social life, but managing her weak bladder was a problem she could not find solutions to. She was reluctant to wear pads because her incontinence only happened on occasions and at first didn't seem that bad. It was certainly worse on exertion and after a few drinks. Gradually however her bladder began to influence more aspects of her life and she was constantly checking how her bladder was. At these times she said to herself 'I'm useless. I can't control myself!' and this made her feel angry and irritable. She found herself making excuses not to go out with her friends, and worrying that she wasn't doing as much playful activity with her granddaughters. She hated saying to them 'You just go and play, Grandma will watch' when they were at the park. Anne wasn't even aware initially that the cause was the worry about her bladder but she began to feel as if she wasn't showing the same interest in the grandchildren and questioned whether she was fit enough to look after them.

Both of these women could be described as having low self esteem. Although they describe their problems in quite different ways and have had the problems for different lengths of time, both women are talking about themselves and their abilities in a negative way.

What is low self-esteem?

Self-esteem is the sense of value and self-worth we have about ourselves. It's not just about how we look, it's a judgment and an evaluation. If our self-esteem is healthy, we can accept our weaknesses and shortcomings because we know we possess strengths and abilities.

Appreciating our characteristics and achievements is a source of psychological well-being. If we have a moderate level of self- esteem we can put negative events down to experience or focus on the times when things have gone better.

What women with bladder problems say about self-esteem

Women say a weak bladder can badly affect their opinions of themselves. Often this relates to feeling out of control, not being able to do things, and no longer feeling attractive. Sometimes women tell themselves they are useless or worthless.

Whatever the situation, labelling ourselves as 'a total failure', 'useless', 'unlovable' can influence our thinking, how we feel and what we do.

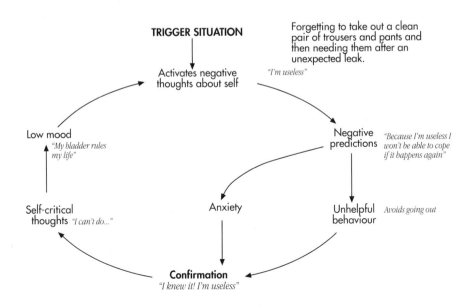

TRIGGER SITUATION

Forgetting to take out a clean pair of trousers and pants and then needing them after an unexpected leak.

Activates negative thoughts about self — *"I'm useless"*

Negative predictions — *"Because I'm useless I won't be able to cope if it happens again"*

Low mood — *"My bladder rules my life"*

Self-critical thoughts *"I can't do..."*

Anxiety

Unhelpful behaviour — *Avoids going out*

Confirmation
"I knew it! I'm useless"

Giving yourself a chance

The basis of low self-esteem is self-criticism. We do something and we tell ourselves we did it wrong or badly. Then we tell ourselves this means we are a stupid or bad person. In people with low self-esteem self-criticism is usually unfair, biased, negative, one-sided, unnecessary, undermining and it makes life worse! Because the criticism comes from within we find ourselves believing it without question.

It has been described as having an 'internal critic': a voice inside us constantly watching what we do and always coming down on the bad side. Imagine the consequences of living with this long term!

The first stage in defeating our internal critic is to give ourselves a fair assessment. This means taking a new look at ourselves and being prepared to let go of some of our old ideas.

THE LOW SELF-ESTEEM ACTION PLAN

Taking a new look at yourself

Accepting yourself the way you are

Defeating self-critical thoughts

Caring for yourself

Thinking about ourselves positively can be hard when we're not used to it. We get used to listening to our self-doubt and do not question it. We start to believe that these thoughts are facts, and not an unhelpful *interpretation* of the facts.

TRY THIS! A self-description sheet

The goal of this exercise is to think about yourself in a positive way.

When you start you may be flooded with familiar thoughts and memories of what has gone wrong in life and all the aspects of yourself you dislike. Let all these thoughts come into your mind and then let them go. Imagine they were on the previous description sheet which now needs updating (see CHARTS section).

Ask a friend or partner to help you. You'll be amazed at all the things they say you won't have thought of. Here's an example.

Margaret is aged 61, and has had a weak bladder for 15 years. Initially she had coped with it but with blood pressure tablets and a worsening of her arthritis she had gradually begun to do less and less. She viewed herself as a failure, physically, socially and personally. She felt anxious and low.

Lets look at what Margaret says about herself (overleaf). What impression do you get of her?

Name **Margaret**

Age **61**

What do you consider your strengths are? **Reliable, resourceful, persistent**

What do other people like about you? **Kindness, thoughtful (remember birthdays), offer others help. Sense of humour, always joking (well, used to before depressed).**

What skills do you have in each of the roles of your life?

Role 1: (eg parent) **Mother - tried to bring the kids up with a sense for right and wrong. Boys are happy, independent adults. I must have done something right.**

Role 2: (eg colleague) **Don't work now, but when I did I was reliable and helpful. Got on with things.**

Role 3: **(eg neighbour) Helpful, not nosey.**

Role 4: **Friend - try to fit in with others plans. Compromise. Thoughtful. Good listener. Have ideas about what to do. Strong in a crisis.**

What do you consider have been achievements in your life? **Bringing up the boys. Good grandmother. Christian values. Going back to college after having the boys.**

What have been difficulties you have overcome? **Divorce from first husband. Getting a new job when I was an older woman. Death of mum when I was 19. Bringing up boys on my own. Bladder - not there yet but trying.**

Margaret needed a lot of encouragement to write these down and felt uncomfortable in case she was boasting or had got it completely wrong. She showed the sheet to a friend who agreed wholeheartedly with it and also added some positives Margaret didn't feel confident enough to write. Each time Margaret called herself a failure she took out her sheet and used it as the starting point for getting a more balanced view.

You may find the list of adjectives in the box below useful to consider.

Adventurous	Enthusiastic	Loving	Responsible
Amusing	Extroverted	Maternal	Self-aware
Attentive	Encouraging	Mature	Self-conscious
Affectionate	Fair	Modest	Sensible
Able	Flexible	Natural	Sensitive
Adaptable	Friendly	Observant	Skilful
Ambitious	Generous	Organised	Sociable
Blunt	Gentle	Original	Strong
Brave	Giving	Practical	Supportive
Calm	Happy	Patient	Sympathetic
Curious	Helpful	Perceptive	Tactful
Caring	Honourable	Persuasive	Tender
Creative	Idealistic	Playful	Thoughtful
Considerate	Imaginative	Pragmatic	Thorough
Cheerful	Independent	Principled	Tough
Complex	Ingenious	Quiet	Trustworthy
Courageous	Innovative	Rational	Understanding
Dependable	Kind	Realistic	Useful
Determined	Knowledgeable	Reasonable	Warm
Dignified	Liberal	Reflective	Wise
Dutiful	Lively	Reliable	Witty
Energetic	Logical	Respectful	

Accepting yourself as you are

Building self-esteem involves actively recognising your skills, abilities and characteristics.

TRY THIS! Positive characteristics chart

Start now by identifying 10 positive characteristics that describe you.
They could be from the list or you can make your own list just by noticing things about yourself over the next week as you go about your normal life.
Put them in a chart or a notebook and tick each characteristic when you notice it in yourself (see CHARTS section).

CHARACTERISTIC	
Thoughtful	✓✓✓
Funny	✓✓
Determined	✓✓✓✓✓✓✓✓
Encouraging	✓✓

Over the next week look at how often these positive characteristics have been around.

How can you criticise yourself so much now in the light of all this evidence?

TRY THIS! Beating the bully and being your own best friend

Defeating self-critical thoughts
Think about your self-critical thoughts as belonging to someone else, an unfair bully for example. Maybe you can identify the bully as a person who has been important in developing your low self-esteem in the first place, for example a disapproving relative who always makes you feel like you've failed. Turning the critical voice into a person can help us fight back.

Fighting Back

Round 1: Calm Yourself The first thing to do is take a few deep breaths. Try the breathing exercises on page 35.

Round 2: Telling the Bully to Shut Up
The next stage is to tell the bully to shut up. Be strong, decisive and powerful. 'Please be quiet' is not as good as 'Shove off you bully!' The goal is to stop your thoughts in their tracks, so you step in with some positives and stop the habit of putting yourself down.
Practice out loud to get a phrase that sums it up for you. Since you'll be saying it silently you can be as frank with your bully as you like!

Round 3: Reaffirming Yourself
You need to repair the harm the bully does. Remind yourself of your basic worth and your efforts to live in a world that is difficult.

Tell yourself:
- I am trying the best I can.
- I am a good person.
- I'm fine the way I am.
- I'm interested in life and trying to make it better.

Once you've stopped the bully you can begin to look at the source of the problem.

TRY THIS! The distressing thoughts action plan (see page 10)

What does your bully say to you? Bullies are persistent and you need to notice when he/she is active.

Once you notice what the bully is saying you may be astonished at how mean your bully is! It's difficult not to believe very familiar put-downs as they become second nature, but there's always another view you can take.

What thinking styles are keeping you down?

What balanced view of yourself can you find?

Remember, we can be positive about ourselves without being boastful. Being modest is often overvalued.

Being your own best friend

As well as beating the bully you can try being a bit kinder to yourself. Think about the role of a best friend:

- Someone who you can rely on to make you feel better when you're down.
- Who values you for who you are, warts and all.
- Who enjoys your company and time.
- Who wants the best for you.
- Who wants to see you happy at all costs
- Who would stick by you through thick or thin.

You might have a friend like this already: it could be this is how your friends see you! Step into your best friend's shoes to mend the damage the bully does. Consider the following questions to help you see another perspective.

QUESTIONS TO ASK YOURSELF

What would your friend say to stop the bully in his/her tracks?

How would your friend describe the events/situation that has made you feel unhappy, anxious or down on yourself?

What positives in the situation would your friend point out to you?

What would your friend say to make you feel better? (This does not have to be factual! Allow your friend some poetic licence to make you feel better!)

What would your friend do next to make you feel better?

If the bully were saying this to your best friend what would you say to them?

Keep asking yourself the question 'Why listen to the bully when you can listen to your best friend?'

Caring for yourself as well as you do for others

Women are generally excellent carers for everyone but often put themselves second: Try to apply some of these skills to yourself.

TRY THIS! Giving yourself pleasures and treats.

Think about as many different ways of enjoying yourself as you can.

Include ways that cost money, are free, are just for yourself, or include the company of others. How often are you giving yourself these pleasures? Could you be doing it more?

Make a commitment to give yourself a treat under the following circumstances: when things go well (a reward); when things go wrong (a comfort); and every day (because you deserve it).

Go with the flow

It's worthwhile saying again that being stressed will not cause your weak bladder. As a reminder genuine stress incontinence is a bladder that leaks when you sneeze, cough or laugh because this exertion puts a physical stress on the muscles that support the neck of the bladder.

What is stress?

For most of the time stress is an essential and healthy part of daily life. It keeps us stimulated and active. However, too much stress can be unhelpful. We can feel tired, overwhelmed and under strain.

Signs of stress can include the following:

Physical symptoms - muscle tension, palpitations, a churning stomach and fatigue.

Emotional symptoms - irritability, worry and less enthusiasm for life.

Cognitive symptoms - poor concentration, indecisiveness, memory changes.

Behavioural symptoms - agitation, lethargy, poor sleep.

What we see as stressful is determined by our previous experience and our coping skills and strategies. There are many ways of coping with problems; there isn't a 'best way'.

The best strategies are those which:

Suit ourselves.

Fit the situation.

We prefer.

Give us the best results.

If we feel we aren't coping, this can be a sign:

We need new strategies.

Those we are using may not fit the situation.

We are using a skill not suited to this particular problem.

When we try and cope with situations we generally have two options of where to focus our energies. We can try to change the problem or we can try to deal with our reaction more effectively.

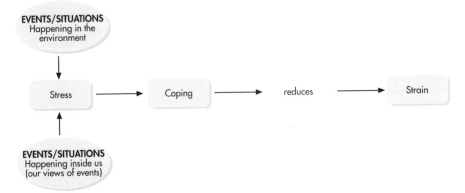

Lorna, 58, had managed her stress incontinence for 10 years quite successfully. Lately however she had begun to experience urge incontinence. She felt damp and uncomfortable and began to worry about her cleanliness. These symptoms had a real effect on her social life, particularly attending dances with her husband. She experienced a headache for days beforehand and felt snappy with her husband when he mentioned their arrangements.

Lorna initially identified what was stressful. Although she coped well with leaks by using good pads, she still fretted about whether their dinner table would be near the toilets or whether she would spend the entire evening trailing backwards and forwards across the dance floor.

Lorna decided to focus (a) coping with the cause of her stress - the new bladder problem and (b) her reaction to it - the stress symptoms of worry, headache and irritability.

She went back to her GP to investigate what could be done for the new problem.

She focused on her reactions by dealing directly with the symptoms of stress - relaxation for the physical aspects - and tried to rationalise her thoughts using the 'distressing thoughts action plan' (see page 10).

She also dealt practically with her worry about where they'd be sitting by contacting the organisers of events and requesting a table near the bathroom. Although it felt like a risk she explained she had a medical condition that meant she liked to have easy access to the toilets. Most organisers were both accommodating and sympathetic.

She also got her husband to accompany her to the toilet on some occasions so it appeared they were taking some time out of the dance together.

The relaxation response

Dr Herbert Benson coined the phrase 'the relaxation response' in the 1970s and noted that as our lives have become more stressful we can lose the skill of relaxation.

TRY THIS: The relaxation response

First, get yourself ready.
A quiet environment - Turn off external distractions and try to switch off internal stresses (worrying thoughts and images).
Choose an object to think about or a 'mantra' - eg repeat a peaceful word to yourself or concentrate on a pleasing feeling.
Adopt a passive attitude - Try to empty all thoughts and distractions from your mind. Although it is inevitable that thoughts may drift into your mind just let them pass to and fro.
Find a comfortable position - Make yourself comfortable enough to remain in the same position for 20 minutes or so.

Once you've done this you can

- Close your eyes
- Relax all the muscles, beginning at your feet and progressing up to your face.
- Breathe in through your nose. Become aware of your breathing. As you breathe out through your mouth say 'one' silently to yourself. Try to empty all thoughts from your mind as you say the word 'one'.
- Continue this for 10 - 20 minutes. When you finish sit quietly for a few minutes, at first with your eyes closed. Do not stand up straight away.
- Do not worry about how relaxed you have been. Let relaxation happen at its own pace. When distracting thoughts come into your mind, ignore them and repeat the word 'one'.

Notice what it's like to be relaxed.

When to use relaxation methods

Like any change we make in life, relaxation will work best if it can fit into our daily routines.

It is helpful to practice regularly, especially when we are trying to master the basic tactics, but we need to find a way to fit it in with the rest of our lifestyle. It's good to set realistic goals.

Rather than going at it hell for leather in the first week and then lapsing for the next month, we need to try the opposite route, of building relaxation into our lives slowly and gradually. A step-by-step approach like this can help build our confidence.

TRY THIS! Getting started

- Make a date in your diary; an appointment with yourself.
- Remind yourself of how much good it's doing you.
- Tell yourself and others you're worth it.
- Enjoy it!

TRY THIS! Keeping a diary

Keep a diary of your activity and progress. Identify the types of relaxation you find most useful and when they give you maximum benefit. (See diary on page 67).

Relaxation methods

Progressive muscle relaxation (PMR)

PMR involves a simple technique of tensing and relaxing the main muscle groups of the body. When you've mastered the basics you can shorten the process and focus on two or three muscle groups; your particular stress points.
Use this basic set of instructions with the muscle groups below:

Shoulders	Shrug up your shoulders towards your ears. Then relax.
Forehead	Scrunch up your eyes and frown. Then relax.
Jaw	Clench your teeth together. Then relax.
Upper back	Pull your shoulders back as though you were trying to touch them behind you. And relax.
Stomach	Pull the muscles of your chest and stomach in and up as if preparing to receive a blow. Relax.
Thighs	Raise your leg about an inch and make your thigh hard. And relax.
Calves	Point your foot and toes forward (do this only briefly as these muscles cramp easily. And relax.

Guided imagery

Guided imagery is a 'distraction' relaxation, which works by replacing tense images and thoughts with pleasant relaxing images. Usually a relaxing scene is described for you to imagine. Some people prefer to build their own personal and detailed picture. Often the image of a pleasant garden, woodland or beach scene is used.

Like getting absorbed in a good film or book it's a useful way to get away from it all.

First of all make yourself as comfortable as possible and when you are ready close your eyes.

Loosen any tight clothing and uncross your arms, legs and ankles. Allow your body to feel supported on your chair or bed. Take a deep breath in through your nose and as you breathe out close your eyes.

Focus for a moment on your breathing, letting relaxation enter your body as you breathe in and letting tension go as you breathe out. Scan your body from the top of your head to the tips of your toes. Relax any tense areas as much as you can and allow yourself to shrink comfortably into the chair or bed, letting tension go and becoming deeply and comfortably relaxed.

Now imagine yourself for a moment walking barefoot along a quiet sandy track. The sun is warm on your face and arms and a gentle cooling breeze is wafting around bringing pleasant smells of the sea and meadow flowers. The sand feels warm and soft underneath your feet.

When you reach the end you can see over the top of the dunes, to the empty beach. The sand is golden in the sunlight and as you look to the horizon you notice the bright blue sky with just a few wisps of white clouds blowing gently across the scene. The sea is calm and turquoise, the sun is sparkling on it as it gently rolls onto the beach, each wave breaking with a gentle white surf. Breathe deeply as you look around the scene. Notice the fresh, cooling air as you breathe it. Notice the salty sensation on your lips. With each breath feel more relaxed and refreshed. As you slowly wander towards the waters edge the sun is warming on your face, the gentle breeze ruffles your hair a little but you feel comfortable and relaxed. Walk along the shoreline for a while taking in the beauty and peace of the scene. Notice the distant calling of the seagulls as they glide in the blue sky, the lapping of the water on the shore, the coolness of the wet sand under your toes.

Feel how peaceful and relaxed you can be. Allow yourself to experience the pleasure and comfort of this beautiful place...

Soon it will be time to return to the dunes, but take a final look around you to remind you how relaxed you are. Take one smell of the sea air. When you are ready take three deep breaths and open your eyes whenever you wish. Remain as relaxed and refreshed as you can. You can return to your special place whenever you wish but for now it is time to go.

Breathing techniques

When we are stressed or anxious our breathing changes to rapid shallow breaths. This is known as over-breathing. The result is a change in the balance of oxygen and carbon dioxide in our blood. This isn't dangerous, but can lead to sensations such as dry mouth, dizziness, and blurred vision.

Re-establishing a normal breathing pattern gets rid of these sensations. Controlling our breathing with counting can be a distraction from worrying thoughts and the physical sensations. Practising these techniques can help you cope with many difficulties such as self consciousness, panic and worry.

TRY THIS! Breathing control

Controlling your breathing is a quick and easy way to relax. It's useful because it quickly reduces anxiety. Try to use it regularly in your life.

Close your eyes. Count to yourself while breathing. Say to yourself 'one thousand' while breathing in and 'two thousand' while breathing out. To slow it down further, say more with each breath.

Quick calming

Quick calming techniques can be used at any time of the day whether you feel stressed or not.

TRY THIS! The Quietening Response

Being mentally active often results in an increase in our physical arousal levels. The idea of the quietening response is to leave ourselves physically more relaxed whilst enabling us to remain alert mentally.

WHAT TO DO:

1. Say to yourself 'active mind, but calm body'.

2. Create an inward smile.

3. At the same time:

- Slow breath in, only slightly exaggerated, to a count of 3 or 4

- Lift ribcage up a few centimetres.

- Notice sensations in the muscles starting from feet, up through legs, stomach, back, shoulders, hands, arms, jaw and eyes (a body scan).

4. Then the following at the same time:

- Slow breath out, slightly longer than the breath in, to a count of 4 or 5. Do not hold your breath and try to keep breathing as naturally as possible.

- Let the ribcage down and think about relaxing some muscles in the body a little.

- Notice any sensations of warmth and comfort and let them flow as you breathe out.

Notice typical daily stressors such as a ringing telephone as a reminder to use the quietening response. While you're starting out routine reminders can be helpful for example, on the hour, or each time you begin a conversation with someone.

Although relaxation itself has been proved useful, no one method is better than another. Choose one you like and have time for, and enjoy it!

What is body image?

Body image is how we see ourselves but it also involves how our bodies feel and what it's like to live within our bodies. A weak bladder can influence how we think we look, and how we feel.

The effects of a weak bladder on body image

A change in body confidence is something many women with a weak bladder say they have to come to terms with. They talk about changes in how they view their physical appearance and this is often linked to wearing a pad.

Women may also say they feel less feminine, healthy, or clean; they may feel their bodies have become unreliable and unhealthy.

The body image action plan

Reviewing your opinion of your body
If your weak bladder has changed your body confidence, try to balance this by renewing your confidence in other areas of your body.

TRY THIS! What image do I have of myself?

Think back to a time before you had a weak bladder. Try to think about attributes and characteristics as well as your appearance when you answer the following questions:

- What did you like then?
- What did you dislike then?
- Which aspects of your body did you pay no attention to? (Body neutral areas?)
- What are the features that other people comment upon?
- What has changed?
- What hasn't changed?
- How healthy did you feel then?

Shift your focus onto what your body can still do or feel. Write a list of all your body parts beginning from your head to your feet. What do you appreciate about them? List the things you can do because this body part is working well.

Reducing attention to appearance and smell
Once we become aware of dissatisfaction with our body we tend to pay it much more attention. This leads to increased self-consciousness, especially because we tend to rely on the use of mirrors to provide us with reassurance.

Women with a weak bladder say they spend a lot of time adjusting their clothing and worrying about their appearance. Regular monitoring has the result of magnifying the importance of small details; the overall picture can be lost. This can lead to preoccupation and self-criticism, especially when it comes to how we appear to others.

Ask yourself the following questions:

- What are the aspects of your body that you monitor more since your weak bladder started?
- Is it always necessary or is some of it a habit?
- What are the effects of this checking for you?

TRY THIS! Estimate before you measure

The next time you're tempted to use a mirror, go through the following steps.

- How comfortable do you feel?

- What are the ways you're judging whether you're OK or not? Use your feelings of comfort and confidence as a guide instead of the mirror.

- Now check how you look. Which method was most reliable? Build up your confidence in your own ability to know your body without relying on the mirror.

Managing fear of smelling

As well as focusing on appearance, women with a weak bladder feel concerned about smell. Most women spend a great deal of time ensuring they don't smell by being scrupulously clean and also masking the possibility of any unwanted odour by using perfumes, deodorants and sprays. However, it can cause self consciousness, so finding a way to limit this worry can be very useful.

TRY THIS! Reducing worries about smell

It's worth checking out if your self-consciousness is really warranted by trying the next 'experiment'.

- Ask a friend or relative what their usual personal hygiene/washing schedule is like i.e. baths and showers per day, deodorant sprays etc. It doesn't matter if they do or do not have a weak bladder (you may not know anyway!).

- Do you wash more or less than them? If it's more try their personal hygiene schedule for a day. Did you notice any differences in odour? Did anyone else? Did you feel differently i.e. felt less clean, worried more?

- If it's a similar schedule to your friend or relative what do you notice about your friend's personal odour?

- If it's less what do you notice about your friend's or relative's personal odour?

The point of the exercise is to help you challenge the view that so much washing is necessary. Often 'feeling dirty' is more about thinking, 'my weak bladder means I'm dirty'. If this is the case for you, treating this as a thought and not a fact may be helpful in reducing worry.

Telling yourself you are OK and believing it

Mirrors give us feedback about our appearance and set us up to focus on our imperfections that others just don't see. So we think the spot on our nose is like a traffic light at stop, but another person has either failed to notice it at all or else doesn't think it matters. If you find this hard to believe, think about the last time you were wearing a new item of clothing you were particularly pleased with. How many people you met that day took any notice? Probably not as many as you would have liked! Most people don't pay as much attention to us as we think.

Dealing with unpleasant body sensations

Having a weak bladder does at times mean we have to deal with unpleasant body sensations such as leakage. It's worth checking you're wearing the pad correctly. Again however, the more attention we pay the more likely we are to notice the sensation. Think about the last time you went shopping and only realised you had a blister on your toe when you got home. Distracting ourselves by paying attention to a different part of our body can reduce distressing thoughts and can make us more comfortable.

Focusing on positive images of body health and fitness

Unfortunately, physical activity is a common trigger for stress incontinence. It's one of the first areas women feel unable to manage.

Has your body image changed because your weak bladder means you do less? How can you do more activity and overcome these restrictions?

TRY THIS! Choose a suitable activity

Swimming and cycling are often mentioned as suitable by women because they are low-impact activities. Cycling shorts are already padded so you may notice your own pads less.

Many women avoid swimming in case they leak in the water. They fear swimming pools use chemicals that mean urine changes the water colour, and everyone will assume they have emptied their bladder in the pool. Be reassured, swimming pools in the UK don't use these chemicals.

For higher impact activities, choose suitable pads - although a lot of women resist buying pads it may be a balance between doing this and not doing your activity. What are the pros and cons of buying suitable products against doing your activity?

IN CONTROL

Overcoming your short-term discomfort about exercise can lead to longer-term gains. When we exercise, our brain produces natural chemicals called endorphins which improve our mood. Add to this your fitness, tone and health, and you have another set of positive aspects to balance against the real distress of living with a weak bladder. Don't give up because your bladder is a problem. Work with it as much as you can and think about your body as a whole rather than just one part.

Blues and loos

A weak bladder can impact on many aspects of our lives, and some of the problems don't have an obvious solution. The result sometimes is a low mood, or depression. If we are low for other reasons, the extra hassle of a weak bladder can make us feel worse. So a weak bladder can be a cause of low mood itself, and an extra problem to manage when we are already down.

What causes low mood?

Depression is a natural reaction to many of life's problems or events, for example the break-up of a relationship, health problems and financial difficulties. What these events have in common is they involve some kind of loss. For health problems like a weak bladder, the losses may not be obvious. Women with a weak bladder say they experience:

Loss of spontaneity and freedom.

Loss of activity.

Loss of feeling feminine and attractive.

The low mood action plan

1. Problem solving

It's important for us to work out where our weak bladder impacts on life and how we feel about it. This way we can work out:

What aspects of the problem we can change and deal with differently.

What aspects of the problem are now part of life and need to be adapted to.

TRY THIS! What problems does my weak bladder cause me?

Over the course of a week, write down in a list all of the problems your weak bladder causes you. Now divide the list into two columns:

   Column A the things you can't change.

   Column B things you think you can change.

With column A notice your thoughts and feelings about this loss. Do this every so often and notice if and how your feelings are changing. How can you reward and comfort yourself for the losses you experience? Check out whether some of these things could be changed in the future if not now.

Sonia's problem list looked like this:

Column A Problems I can't do anything about	Column B Problems I could do something about
Loss issue: Can't get a full night's sleep anymore. Can't do any walking without a pad. So much washing!	Not going out on trip with friends
What can I do? Need to acknowledge the unfairness of this. Feel sad, angry and fed up about it at times without criticising myself as "self pitying".	What can I do?

Although Sonia was upset by what she wrote in Column A she understood why she felt low. She realised she was missing her spontaneity. It also prompted her to consider how much adjustment she had made. Although she felt it was unfair she had to manage a weak bladder, she had worked out good practical methods to help her feel in control.

You can put what you've written in Column B into the next stage: Problem solving.

Problem solving has a number of steps; some may seem very obvious but if you're 'stuck' with a problem that seems to have no answers it can be very useful to go through the steps.

TRY THIS! Problem solving

Step 1	Define the problem. Be as precise as you can. "Living with a weak bladder" needs more explanation such as "Leaking if I reach for something in the supermarket".
Step 2	Generate all the possible solutions, however outlandish, bizarre or impossible they may sound.
Step 3	Put each of the options on a pros and cons list. This helps give a sense of what "feels" like the best solution as well as what is possible, realistic and rational.
Step 4	Choose the solution which best suits you.
Step 5	Think through possible hurdles and help you can get to overcome them.
Step 6	Write a plan if you need more help. This is especially useful when we are depressed because breaking large tasks into small sections makes them easier to start and finish (a bit like following a complicated recipe).
Step 7	Check out whether it has worked (evaluate).

Now look at Sonia's table

Step 1	*Problem*	Leaking if I reach for something at work or in the supermarket.
Step 2	*Possible solutions*	Wear a pad. Forget about it - come home and change. Don't reach in the supermarket. Go to GP/Nurse. Magic wand.
Step 3	*Pros and Cons of options*	**Eg. Option 1: Go to Nurse/GP** **Pros** · **Cons** Could give me some help. · Embarrassing At least I'll know what the · Difficult to get an appointment options are. **Eg. Option 2: Wear a pad** **Pros** · **Cons** Can change it · Annoying Stops staining · Expensive
Step 4	*Choose an option to try*	Go to Nurse/GP
Step 5	*Overcome hurdles*	Ask Jane to cover for me at lunch so I can pop home to ring for an appointment.
Step 6	*Plan further*	Ring on next day off. Get nurse's name from receptionist. Find out if they do a "Well Woman Clinic" an book for then.
Step 7	*Did it work*	Appointment for after work on Thursday to talk to nurse. See where to go from here.

Dealing with distressing thoughts

The distressing thought action plan is especially useful with the negative thoughts that accompany depression.

Phyllis had been low in herself for about eight weeks. She had been sleeping badly, weeping at the slightest thing and feeling unable to cope. She thought to herself 'I'm useless to everyone now I am getting older - the world's a rotten place anyway. What is there left to live for?'. When her daughter gently asked 'what's wrong mum?' Phyllis realised she had been down for a long time but a new event related to her weak bladder had been the final straw. She had recently been discharged from the hospital's Physiotherapy Department because she had been taught all she needed to know to manage her pelvic floor exercises. However, she felt she had lost the support of the Physio and she just had to get on with it because nothing more could be done. In chatting it through with her daughter she recognised her sadness about having to live with a weak bladder and what this meant to her, but also the way she was looking at the discharge was making her feel worse. It was up to her to practise the pelvic floor exercises to maintain her improvements, but the physiotherapist had reassured her she could contact the department at any time if she needed further help.

Coping with body shame

Some women with bladder problems feel ashamed of themselves for not being able to control their bladder or for feeling their bladders are letting them down.

TRY THIS! Reducing shame

Notice if you feel ashamed. What are the thoughts you have about your bladder at these times? Put these thoughts into the distressing thoughts action plan. Where are the unhelpful thinking styles? What challenges can you make?

Work out which of the coping styles you usually use to cope with shame:

- Withdrawal.
- Avoidance.
- Hiding.
- Over compensating.

How can you make a small change to one of these? Using the problem solving techniques (page 44) will help if is hard to get started.

Coping with guilt

Feeling guilty usually comes from a view that we have done something we shouldn't have or not done something we should have. Women with a weak bladder say they feel guilty about 'not looking after themselves'. Often this is about not doing pelvic floor exercises.

However, while pelvic floor exercises are well-known now, they were not so well-publicised or encouraged in ante-natal care or public health campaigns a decade ago, so many women have missed out on this information until recently. The good news is that starting anytime can help. Healthy guilt can motivate us to put something right. Sometimes however guilt can be unhealthy in that we feel bad about something which we don't need to e.g. eating one cream cake when we are on a diet.

'In my experience and that of other women I've spoken to, doctors tend to say immediately 'have you done your pelvic floor exercises?' This is interpreted by us as 'if only you'd done your pelvic floor exercises you wouldn't be in this situation in the first place!' Caroline, 39.

TRY THIS! Challenging guilt

Answer the following question:

I feel guilty because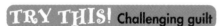

- -

Now subject your guilty feeling to the following questions:

- Have I done this knowingly or on purpose to hurt myself or others? If so what could I do to put it right?

- What is an appropriate amount of repairing or remorse? Have I done enough to be forgiven?

- What can I learn to prevent myself making this mistake again?

- Am I labelling myself as bad because of one small mistake?

- Am I expecting myself to always get everything absolutely right?

- Am I working with unrealistic standards for myself? (Shoulds, oughts and musts).

Forgiving yourself

Now you've taken these into account, look through the section on being your own best friend. Find a way to let the guilt go by being kinder to yourself.

Coping with physical symptoms

Sleep

Sleep disturbance is an extremely common symptom with both a weak bladder and low mood. It can be the case that if your bladder wakes you, your thoughts prevent you from settling back to sleep. Common patterns of sleep disturbance include:

- Failing to get off to sleep.
- Waking early in the morning.
- Waking during the night.

TRY THIS! Getting back to sleep

Making yourself comfortable

- Make sure your bedroom is as comfortable and soothing as you can. Try to avoid using it as an office, a laundry room, a TV lounge. All these will attract your attention if you're having difficulty sleeping.

- Keep the temperature comfortable; keep a window open for fresh air.

- Make your bed as comfortable as you can. A mattress cover can make a difference by reducing your worries about leaks. A designer bed pad which has a 'feel dry' surface and absorbs any leaks may help by making you feel more comfortable and secure.

- Fix a reasonable regular bedtime. Get yourself into a soothing routine.

- Avoid eating a large meal before bedtime.

- Avoid caffeine drinks, but don't avoid fluids.

If you do get up in the night

- Try to keep your bed just for sleeping. If you find you're tossing and turning, sit in a different room until you begin to feel sleepy again.

- Don't keep checking how long you've been trying to get to sleep; it only adds to the pressure.

- Avoid switching on the lights; bright light may make you more alert.

- Socket night lights can be useful.

- Try to prepare for an accident or need to change a pad. Keep wet wipes, a towel, a new pad and dry clothing together in an easily accessible place such as a linen basket in the bathroom.

Try to keep angry thoughts to a minimum. Tell yourself you'll deal with it in the morning. Work out a reassuring thought to tell yourself during the night: 'I've dealt with it well. I'm clean and comfortable now so settle back down'.

If you have a bad night's sleep

Tell yourself it need not happen again and again: you can break the pattern.

Don't lie in to catch up. Being tired for the day may be unpleasant but it may also help you sleep better tonight.

Try not to cat nap.

Dealing with low activity levels

First, get an accurate picture of how much you're doing and how much you would like to do.

TRY THIS! An activity diary

Keeping a diary for a week helps you to see how you're spending your time. Write in it as you go. If you leave it until the evening or the next day your memory may let you down. Include everything. It's easy when you're low to discount small things as irrelevant. Every activity counts at this stage.

With a complete picture of what you've done, answer the following questions:

Was this a typical week?

If yes, how?

Which of the activities was easiest to accomplish?

Which was the most difficult?

Which gave you a sense of satisfaction?

Which didn't?

Which did you enjoy?

Which would you like to see more of in a typical week?

What next?

Notice your danger spots. Are there regular times when you do less?

Either schedule a rest or plan an activity. See which gives the best results.

> Do you find if you get going early in the day you can do more?

> Does making arrangements to do activities with other people help?

> Are you underestimating how much you do?

It's important to add more pleasures and treats when you're low than getting tasks and jobs completed. As with most things a balance is best. Make sure you aren't undervaluing your achievements. Doing a basket of ironing may not seem like much but reward yourself for the effort it took to get it done.

Talk about your problem

If you need more . . .

If the above techniques don't help or if your mood is particularly low you may need to consult your GP. Anti-depressant medication may be prescribed.

Your GP may be also able to refer you on to appropriate specialist help such as a clinical psychologist, counsellor or mental health team.

Anxiety is humankind's oldest survival mechanism. The anxiety response developed to alert us to danger and give us the opportunity to protect ourselves. Anxiety itself is a good thing. It's only when it becomes excessive or out of control that it's unhelpful. Even then it's not physically dangerous to us, but because it feels so dreadful it can affect us psychologically.

The anxiety response is sometimes known as the 'fight, flight and freeze' response. The body floods with adrenaline which has an immediate impact on all the body's major physical systems which make fighting, running or freezing possible. It makes the heart beat faster to pump blood around the body so it can feed the muscles with more oxygen. We breathe quicker to oxygenate the blood. Our muscles tense ready for action.

Other body systems, which are less urgently needed to ensure our survival, are temporarily shut down. We stop digesting food and we feel the need to empty our bladder and bowels.

Of course we no longer face the same physical dangers, but we respond in the same physical way to any events we see as threatening to us. Usually events which we now see as threatening involve a threat to our psychological well-being, such as how others see us rather than a physical threat.

Hannah's story
Hannah had been invited to a family wedding and began to feel anxious because she thought she would be unable to get to a toilet if she needed one. She imagined having to sneak down the aisle during the ceremony and everyone would be staring and wondering what she was doing. She felt sure they would know she had a bladder problem and they would think she was spoiling the ceremony. Two weeks before the wedding her daughter asked her what she planned to wear. She then began to imagine a worse scenario where she had 'an accident' and had to leave with a stain on her pale coloured wedding suit. When she imagined this scenario she became hot and bothered, her legs turned to jelly and her heart started racing. She had an immediate thought 'I can't cope! I can't go!' and became upset and tearful because the scenario seemed so real.

Hannah's story above demonstrates some facts about anxiety:

1. We can have the same reaction whether we are in real danger or if we *imagine* we are in danger or under threat.

2. The reaction affects us in the four major ways:
   Emotionally We feel frightened, nervous, panicky, anxious and worried.
   Physically Heart rate increases, we can sweat, tremble or shake, our stomach churns (butterflies), and we experience tension in the muscles (jelly legs). We also have an increased urge to go to the toilet.
   Cognitively Our thoughts, beliefs, images and memories become focused on the negative and threatening and we begin to scan the immediate situation for other dangers.
   Behaviourally We may cope by avoiding situations which we predict are threatening and leave situations in which we think something disastrous has happened.

3. It's our *interpretation* that we're in danger or are facing a threat which causes the anxiety. In reality we are usually quite safe.

4. Although the symptoms feel awful at the time, they can't do us any physical harm and do pass quickly.

5. We can control anxious symptoms by putting certain strategies into practice.

So far we have been talking about general anxiety. Sometimes people with this describe themselves as 'worriers' and find many events or situations cause their symptoms to worsen.

Another form of anxiety which is common to women with bladder problems is *panic attacks.*

Look at the vicious cycle opposite that happened to Hannah. As in Hannah's case, thoughts can be as powerful as real dangers in the environment.

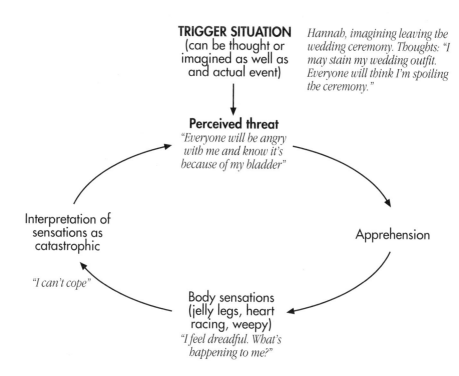

TRIGGER SITUATION (can be thought or imagined as well as and actual event)

Hannah, imagining leaving the wedding ceremony. Thoughts: "I may stain my wedding outfit. Everyone will think I'm spoiling the ceremony."

Perceived threat
"Everyone will be angry with me and know it's because of my bladder"

Interpretation of sensations as catastrophic

"I can't cope"

Apprehension

Body sensations (jelly legs, heart racing, weepy)
"I feel dreadful. What's happening to me?"

When we feel anxious we are likely to do four things at the same time which make us feel as if the danger is real.

    1. We **overestimate** the chance something bad will happen.

    2. We **overestimate** how bad it will be if it does happen.

    3. We **underestimate** our own ability to cope.

    4. We **underestimate** the help and support that is available from others

In Hannah's case she:

    Overestimated the probability of needing to leave the church and that she would have an accident.

    Underestimated all the practical things she could do in advance to prevent the problem.

    Underestimated how supportive others would be.

Understanding the way anxiety starts and continues can be useful in itself, but there are many other techniques we can use to help. Being aware of your thoughts is especially useful for anxiety, panic and worry.

TRY THIS! Why am I worrying?

Work out if there are unhelpful thinking styles. Use the following questions to help you challenge unhelpful thinking.

QUESTIONS TO ASK

Is it reasonable for me to worry about this situation or am I worrying for worrying sake?

How likely is it that the worst event could happen? (Give it a score out of 10).

How bad would it be if it did happen?

What help and support could I get from other people if it happened?

Let's go back to Hannah. Having identified her distressing thoughts as 'I may stain my wedding outfit' she subjected her thoughts to the questions in the box above. Her answers were as follows:

1. It's a reasonable worry as an accident would stain the suit and people could see. But I've never had an accident before because I take precautions. I'm not used to wearing pale clothes. I could see if I can get used to it before the wedding and if I can't, I'll wear something I do feel comfortable in.

2. It's unlikely. Maybe 1/10. It's a possibility with a weak bladder but with pads or special pants I'm OK.

3. It would be absolutely dreadful if I did have an accident at the wedding. I can't imagine anything worse, but it's unlikely anyway. In any case all eyes would be on the bride not me!

4. I'd do what I've always planned to do - get changed. I always carry around spare clothing. The wedding is at a hotel so there are bound to be facilities.

5. My husband and daughter will both be there to help. If I had stained my suit I know my daughter would tell me and then help me find somewhere to change. She would certainly run and get my clothes and help me get to a suitable place with the least possible fuss. There's lots of distractions at weddings anyway, what with babies crying and children getting bored.

By anwering these questions Hannah saw her fears and anxieties had taken hold, but she could get them under control.

Controlling over-breathing

When we panic we can start over-breathing (or hyperventilating, as it's sometimes known).

TRY THIS! Stopping over-breathing

First of all work out the difference between shallow breathing and deep breathing.

Place one hand on your chest and one hand on your stomach. Take in a deep breath and allow your chest to rise and swell. This is deep breathing and is the type of breathing you should aim for in a panic attack if you're over-breathing.

Now:

Breathe in through your nose to a count of three, raising your chest and stomach.

Breathe out through your mouth to a count of four or five.

Don't hold your breath before you breathe out. Keep your breathing regular.

Aim to take seven to 12 breaths per minute (one breath counts as a breath-in and a breath-out).

Keep your breathing slow and regular.

Practise this regularly when you aren't in a panic situation so it's a well learnt skill.

Facing the things you fear

If we face fears gradually in small manageable steps we can learn situations aren't as frightening. Our anxiety decreases as our confidence increases.

TRY THIS! Setting goals and graded practice

First of all write down one situation you're worried about and want to change. Set something which you think could be within your reach if you could overcome your fear.

I am fearful/worried/panicky about _ _ _ _ _ _ _ _ _ _ _ _ _ _ _ _ _ _

_ _

Now set the goal

I would like to be able to_ _

_ _

The next task is to think about the steps that could take you towards this goal. Begin by writing down something you can already do. Next think about something that is a bit harder than this but that could be in reach with help.

Write down steps in this way beginning with the easiest and ending with the most difficult. This list is sometimes called a 'fear ladder', because it starts on the bottom rung with what is manageable and you take a step at a time until you get to the top, which is the most difficult step.

Barbara wrote the following as her fear:

'Travelling in other peoples cars for more than 10 minutes in case I need the loo or stain their car seats'.

Her fear ladder looked like this, with the goal at the top and the easiest step at the bottom.

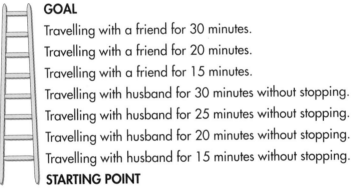

GOAL

Travelling with a friend for 30 minutes.

Travelling with a friend for 20 minutes.

Travelling with a friend for 15 minutes.

Travelling with husband for 30 minutes without stopping.

Travelling with husband for 25 minutes without stopping.

Travelling with husband for 20 minutes without stopping.

Travelling with husband for 15 minutes without stopping.

STARTING POINT

Barbara could already travel with her husband because he would stop when asked so she began setting steps on her ladder which were slightly more difficult but still possible.

Practise calming skills to help you manage the anxiety.

Choose a time to start when you can practise regularly and often.

Reward yourself and get others to recognise your achievements.

Keep repeating the same step until the anxiety has gone and then go onto the next step.

Barbara realised it was only anxiety preventing her from staying in the car. She could hold her bladder for that long in the house so she knew she could do it in the car. She was delighted she was now in control of her bladder again.

Distraction

Another method of coping is to occupy your mind with more pleasant images and thoughts. Although we can think of many things at the same time we can break cycles of worry by thinking pleasant thoughts instead of worries.

TRY THIS! Distraction techniques

Physical exercise **Walking around the block, walking up and down a corridor to get a drink can break the cycle by removing you from the environment in which you were worrying. Tidying a room, tidying your handbag, sorting washing, cleaning a window are all other ideas.**

Re-focusing **Focusing your attention on something interesting in the environment takes your mind off your immediate worries. For example, Miriam always bought a programme at the theatre to occupy her before the play started. This meant she was distracted instead of worrying whether she had enough time for another trip to the loo.**

Imagery and mental athletics **Remembering previously enjoyable times, reciting a poem, counting backwards in 3s from 417.**

Yvonne kept a key-ring with a photo of her children on a ride at Alton Towers in her bag. When she began to panic she experienced a real uplift from looking at their joyful faces.

Love me, love my bladder

Many women say their weak bladder has affected close relationships. Often this is because of how they see themselves, because they are afraid others will be rejecting or disapproving. However women also describe how they get excellent support from husbands, partners and friends and say how they only wish they had shared the problem sooner!

Sharing your difficulties with family and friends

TRY THIS! Telling others

Giving a simple explanation of your condition is a good way to start.

> 'My doctor says it is very common for women to experience this after they have had a baby'.

> 'I've stopped going to the gym because I leak when I jump'.

> 'The news is good, I have already started some treatment'.

Begin by telling them something about the problem in general and then if you feel you want to you can say something about your specific problems, experiences or feelings. Describing your problems can help you to acknowledge your own feelings and put your family and friends at ease. It also corrects any myths, fears or assumptions others may have about your bladder condition. The chances are that they know someone else who has similar problems.

Refresh your own knowledge of how your bladder works by re-reading the earlier sections and focusing on your condition. Being experts about our own bladder gives the message to others that we are in control of the situation. Our apparent confidence will put others at ease.

> Reassure yourself and your family that you have a genuine and common condition which can affect as many as one in three women of all ages.

> Be positive. If you have started treatment it may cure you completely or will certainly make your life easier to manage. If you haven't yet been to see anyone there are plenty of other things you can do to help yourself.

> Plan in advance what you wish to say so that if you have an unwelcome interruption you won't get flustered.

You may find our **SHARE** list useful:

START Prepare by getting the facts together.

HELP Remind yourself that others can help you if you let them.

ADVANCE Plan who you are going to talk to first, where you are going to talk and how you are going to talk before you do it.

REHEARSE/RELAX/REWARD Calm yourself, practise what you want to say in a safe setting and give yourself a treat afterwards.

EVALUATE What went well? What would you change next time if you told someone else?

Disruptions to family life

Heidi's son had recently split up with his partner and returned home to live. Heidi had an overactive bladder but was coping extremely well. She was able to dash to the loo in time. Problems began when her son was spending long periods in the bathroom in the morning, bathing and shaving. He could not understand why his mother, an easy-going woman, became so agitated about the amount of time he was spending in the bathroom. Heidi had to get up several times at night and each time she walked past her son's bedroom the floorboards would creak and she would feel anxious. 'I feel like I'm walking on eyelashes' she told her friend. As her anxiety and embarrassment increased she decided she would have to tell her son about her bladder. His immediate reaction was to give his mother a big hug.

These are common problems in busy households with one bathroom. However agreeing some new rules about how to accommodate your needs can be helpful as well. In addition, why not:

Try using a commode or potty as an alternative to the loo.

Break up the bathroom routine so each person has a few minutes each.

Distract yourself by doing something else.

Children and Younger Adults

Louisa had mixed incontinence since the birth of her third child. Generally she managed well, but her eldest child, aged 9 years, had begun to ask why she went to the toilet so much. Louisa had managed to evade this questions until recently, but he had been particularly insistent that she was a parent helper on the next school trip. Louisa knew she could not last the two hours on the bus trip without a stop, but did not know where to begin in explaining it to her son.

Explaining to children and younger adults poses different concerns for women, but it is again a common problem. Looking after grandchildren can involve physical activities, which cause more leaks. As gaining bladder and bowel control is the earliest task we set children, and they are often still scolded for 'accidents', it is not difficult to see why we feel bad as adults for the supposed 'lack of control' that a weak bladder causes us. Sometimes laughing it off can be the best way to diffuse difficult questions. 'Ever since my grandson called my catheter a pea shooter', said Ellen, 'I have felt more relaxed about wearing it and I have even been able to joke about it with family and friends'.

As with other tricky subjects for children:

Start with the child's understanding of how the body works.

Use an analogy, such as a leaking tap.

Reassure them it is not dangerous or painful but natural and manageable.

Younger women may need to know that it is not inevitable for women, and you can tell them about the role of pelvic floor muscle exercises in prevention.

Husbands and partners

Many women talk about feeling 'undesirable', 'unattractive' and 'unlovable'. Partners may also have their own anxieties and may be unsure how to respond to you. A cuddle, a hug, a few words of reassurance can make a huge difference.

Some common problems during sex

A common fear for partners is about wetting during sex. A leak is not always urine however. During sex some women pass fluid from the large network of tubes which surround the vagina or leak seminal fluid after sex.

Sometimes the bladder muscle contracts during sexual excitement causing a leak of urine. Medication is available which may reduce this if it's a problem for you. However, be reassured urine is not infectious.

If you're worried about leaking, you can increase your confidence by lying on an absorbent sheet - the 'satin looking' sexy materials absorb leaks and can be machine washed and dried. It may also help if you don't drink a lot of alcohol or cola just before you have sex.

Painful sex

Some women are so worried about having an accident, they become tense and this can lead to a problem called 'vaginismus', a tensing of the vaginal muscles which can result in painful sex. Use the relaxation and calming techniques in the stress and relaxation section on page 33.

Talking together about your feelings and fears
The following may help:

Changing your normal positions for love-making

Many couples find caressing each other and lying close together gives them the sexual satisfaction they need.

Keep sleeping in your double bed.

Old problems in new relationships
Beginning a new relationship raises normal issues of trust and intimacy. This can be particularly difficult if we feel our weak bladders have been the cause of a breakdown in previous relationships. For many reasons women with a weak bladder often comment on anxiety about beginning a new relationship.

Working out when and how to tell a partner is often a worry to women. Often many women may think that they have hidden the problem well only to find their partner realised long before and does not see it as a problem. Often a partner's questions or interest is simply so they can better understand the problem. It is helpful to tell yourself that it is only when they understand more about your situation that they can offer you the support and help you may need. There is a useful distinction to make between secrecy and privacy. Hiding your bladder problems may not be possible but managing yourself to retain some privacy and dignity is fine. Set the rules to suit yourself and then be clear about them with your partner.

- *Be prepared to negotiate. Although you may prefer to sleep in a separate room because you fear it will disturb your partner, allow them to have their say rather than making the decision alone. Maybe they would prefer a cuddle and a hug and don't care that you get up in the night.*

- *Most people are happy to follow reasonable rules and expectations if you tell them what they are, such as privacy in the bathroom or single beds at night.*

- *Remind yourself men have problems too!*

- *Lack of information is a key problem; showing others you know how to manage the problem will help to guide your new partner.*

- *Many new partners will be relieved it is nothing serious.*

- *One in three women experience problems. Your new partner may already know about weak bladders from other friends and relatives.*

Relationships can and do break down for many reasons. Talking to someone in confidence about your problems can help get life back into perspective. Organisation such as RELATE and Marriage Care have specially trained counsellors who can help. Their telephone numbers are included on page 64.

Who can help

Contact your GP, practice nurse or district nurse. They may then refer you to other health professionals.

Investigations and treatments for medical conditions are available free on the NHS. The range of services and products vary according to where you live. Where you may have to pay for the service we advise you check the cost includes VAT.

Health professionals who can help

Your GP can diagnose your symptoms, prescribe treatments and refer to a specialist.

Continence Advisor - a nurse with training in bladder problems.

Urotherapist - a physiotherapist with skills in treating pelvic floor muscles.

Urogynaecologist - a doctor with training in bladder and gynaecological problems.

Clinical Psychologist - a therapist who treats the emotional aspect of incontinence.

Occupational Therapist - offers practical help with devices and aids if you are having difficulty reaching the toilet in a hurry.

To boldly go...

This section gives national contacts. They may be able to suggest local contacts. You may have to pay for some of these services.

British Association of Behavioural & Cognitive Psychotherapies
Tel/Fax : 01254 875277
List of cognitive behavioural therapists accredited by the organisation.

British Psychological Society
Tel: 0116 254 9568
Provides a directory of chartered clinical psychologists who are employed in the NHS and privately.

Continence Foundation Helpline
Tel: 0845 345 0165 Monday-Friday 9.30am-4.30pm
Specialist nurses offering free advice about your bladder problems.

Incontact
Tel: 020 7700 7035
Support group for people with bladder and bowel problems.

interstitial cystitis support group (icsg)
Tel: 01908 569 169
Support group.

Marriage Care
Tel: 020 7371 1341
24 hour answerphone
Free confidential service to anyone with relationship difficulties.

PromoCon
Tel: 0161 834 2001
Free independent information on the range of products for bladder control.

RADAR (Royal Association for Disability and Rehabilitation)
12 City Forum, 250 City Road, London EC1 8AF
Tel: 020 7250 3222
Provides information on the NKS for keys and directories to toilets.

Relate
Tel: 01788 573 241 (24 hour ansaphone)
Confidential service to anyone with relationship difficulties.

Further reading

Feeling Good - The New Mood Therapy. Burns DM, 1989, Plume/Penguin, USA.
The Feeling Good Handbook. Burns DM, 1992, Avon Books, New York.

The 'Overcoming' Series
Overcoming low self esteem. Melanie Fennell, (1999).
Overcoming social anxiety and shyness. Gillian Butler, (1999).
Overcoming anxiety. Helen Kennerly, (1999).
Overcoming depression. Paul Gilbert, (1999).
Overcoming panic. Derrick Silore & Vijaya Manicovasagar, (1999).
Available mail order, Robinson Publishing 020 7938 3830 or most bookshops.

A Woman in Your Own Right - Assertiveness and You. Anne Dickson (1982),
Quartet Books, London.

The Family Doctor Guide to: Urinary Incontinence in Women. Dr Philip Toozs-
Hobson & Prof. Linda Cardozo. (1999), Dorling Kindersley Limited, London.

Bladder and Bowel Problems. Incontact (1999). Free from InContact.

Choosing Products for Bladder and Bowel Control. Ricability/Promocon 2001,
(1999), available free from Promocon (SAE required).

Diaries and charts

This section contains the charts and diaries referred to throughout the Guide. Adapt them if you need to, so you record what is helpful for you.

Some people find carrying a notebook or diary easier than sheets of paper. Some women eventually feel the diaries are unnecessary. We encourage you to keep them in the first instance however until you get used to the methods.

Relaxation Diary

Day, date and time	Relaxation method	Tension rating		Comments
		Before	After	

Self description sheet

Name

Age

What do you consider your strengths are?

What do other people like about you?

What skills do you have in each of the roles of your life?

Role 1 (eg. parent)

Role 2 (eg. colleague)

Role 3 (eg. neighbour)

Role 4:

What do you consider have been achievements in your life?

What have been difficulties you have ovecome?

The distressing thoughts diary

Event/situation	Feelings	Thoughts	Behaviour	Unhelpful thinking styles	Alternative balanced thoughts

Activity diary

Time	Monday	Tuesday	Wednesday	Thursday	Friday	Saturday	Sunday

Bladder training diary

Please ✔ each time you pass urine
✗ each time you are wet

Time	Monday	Tuesday	Wednesday	Thursday	Friday	Saturday	Sunday

Drinks diary

Please record everything you drink for 3 days, indicating whether you used a glass, cup or mug.

Day 1			Day 2			Day 3		
Time	Amount	Type	Time	Amount	Type	Time	Amount	Type